The Gift

by Caleb Davis
illustrated by Matthew Ziegler

Practice Pre-Decodable 2

Mc Graw Hill Education

Bothell, WA • Chicago, IL • Columbus, OH • New York, NY

MHEonline.com

Send all inquiries to:
McGraw-Hill Education
8787 Orion Place
Columbus, OH 43240

ISBN: 978-0-02-132198-8
MHID: 0-02-132198-1

Printed in the United States of America.

8 9 10 CTM 23